Headhunters
and
Hummingbirds

Also by Robert McCracken Peck

A CELEBRATION OF BIRDS:
THE LIFE AND ART OF LOUIS AGASSIZ FUERTES

Headhunters
and
Hummingbirds

AN EXPEDITION INTO ECUADOR

BY

Robert McCracken Peck

WALKER AND COMPANY NEW YORK

First published in the United States of America
in 1987 by the Walker Publishing Company, Inc.

Published simultaneously in Canada by John Wiley & Sons
Canada, Limited, Rexdale, Ontario.

Portions of this book first appeared in slightly different
form in The Philadelphia Inquirer Magazine, April 6, 1986.
Permission to use this material is gratefully acknowledged.

Library of Congress Cataloging-in-Publication Data

Peck, Robert McCracken, 1952–
Headhunters and hummingbirds.

Bibliography: p.
Includes index.
Summary: A journalist-photographer describes his
adventures on an expedition for ornithological research
into the Cutucú Mountains of inner Ecuador.
1. Birds—Ecuador—Cutucú Mountains—Juvenile
literature. 2. Scientific expeditions—Ecuador—
Cutucú Mountains—Juvenile literature. 3. Peck,
Robert McCracken, 1952–   —Journeys—Ecuador—
Cutucú Mountains—Juvenile literature. 4. Cutucú
Mountains (Ecuador)—Description and travel—Juvenile
literature. [1. Cutucú Mountains (Ecuador)—Description
and travel. 2. Scientific expeditions—Ecuador.
3. Birds—Ecuador] I. Title.
QL689.E2P43   1987   508.866'4   86-15908
ISBN 0-8027-6645-5
ISBN 0-8027-6646-3 (Reinforced)

Printed in the United States of America

10 9 8 7 6 5 4 3 2 1

Book designed by Laurie McBarnette

In memory of

LOUISE CATHERWOOD CHAPLIN

Contents

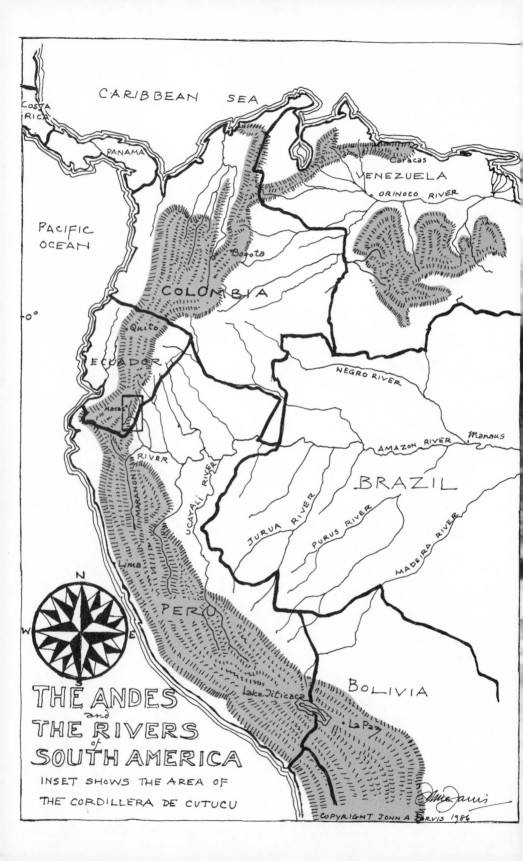

CARIBBEAN SEA

COSTA RICA

PANAMA

PACIFIC OCEAN

VENEZUELA

Caracas

ORINOCO RIVER

Bogota

COLOMBIA

0°

Quito

ECUADOR

Macas

NEGRO RIVER

AMAZON RIVER

Manaus

RIVER

MARAÑON RIVER

UCAYALI RIVER

BRAZIL

JURUA RIVER

PURUS RIVER

MADEIRA RIVER

Lima

PERU

N

W   E

S

THE ANDES
and
THE RIVERS
of
SOUTH AMERICA

INSET SHOWS THE AREA OF

THE CORDILLERA DE CUTUCU

Lake Titicaca

BOLIVIA

La Paz

COPYRIGHT JOHN A. JARVIS 1986

Foreword

From the twisting blacktop road that links Mendez and Sucùa with the larger towns of Macas and Puyo to the north, Ecuador's Cordillera de Cutucu looks like any other Andean mountain ridge. But to a team of American naturalists who penetrated its forbidden borders for the first time in 1984, the Cutucu are anything but ordinary.

I was fortunate to be a member of that team, or at least I feel so now, looking back on the trip from the comfort and safety of home. I didn't feel so fortunate the day we learned we'd been targeted for attack by head-shrinking Indians, or when our food supplies ran low and we had to live on monkey meat and hummingbirds.

Acknowledgments

The success of the expedition described in this book is a testament to the remarkable personalities of the many people involved. I am grateful to Frank Gill and Robert Ridgely, co-leaders of the expedition, for inviting me to participate, and to the administration of the Academy of Natural Sciences of Philadelphia for granting me the time to do so. The individuals most directly involved with the expedition are featured in the main body of the story. Each added an important dimension to the undertaking and collectively made the many hardships of the expedition easier to endure. I was fortunate to have experienced the wild diversity of the Cutucu in such company. The bonds of comradery thus formed will last a lifetime.

All of us who participated in the expedition are indebted to the Catherwood Foundation, Mrs. Edward Cassard, Mr. and Mrs. Frederick W. G. Peck, and Mr. and Mrs. Henry Woolman for their confidence and generous financial support. We are also grateful to the government of Ecuador and our colleagues at the Museo Ecuatoriano de Ciencias Naturales in Quito, without whose assistance we could never have undertaken this project.

I am pleased that Beth Walker suggested the idea of a book, and that Barbara Bates agreed to serve as my editor. Beth has been unflagging in her support, and Barbara has made a pleasure of the difficult process of turning a story into a book. Two others have played an important part in shaping the manuscript as well. My thanks to Jocelyn Kelley and Mary Dolack for their countless hours of careful reading, constructive criticism, encouragement, and support. Finally to my colleagues at the Academy and elsewhere, who patiently reviewed and verified the accuracy of the text, I am grateful.

1

Leaving Civilization

"This is it," said Bob Ridgely, his voice barely audible above the roar of the river. "From here on we'll be in Jívaro country."

A long, swaying cable bridge stretched out above the river border like a skinny trampoline. Behind us lay the dry, rutted road from Logroño, a frontier town so small most of Ecuador's mapmakers had failed to notice it. Before us lay the wide Upano River valley, its lush vegetation unbroken by roads or houses. Here the map read JÍVARO (SHUAR) TRIBAL LANDS and, in somewhat smaller print, UNEXPLORED. This was the land of the head-shrinking Indians, whose fierce warlike ways had become legendary long before the rest of Ecuador was tamed.

The valley made a gentle U-shaped sweep from the river to a narrow, rounded ridge, then dropped to begin a series of rippled hills, each higher than the one before it: up, then down, then up again, until the lines

1

Mark Robbins crosses the great swinging bridge that spans the Upano River. Behind him lies Logroño and the settled agricultural lands of southeastern Ecuador. Ahead lie the tribal lands of the Jívaro Indians and the unknown jungles of the Cutucu.

3

were hard to see. The last became impossible to distinguish from the ones before them and the billowing clouds beyond. These were the Cordillera de Cutucu, the "mountains of moss" we had traveled so far to explore.

Bob Ridgely shifted his shotgun from one shoulder to the other and jerked his shoulders to adjust the weight of his pack. I offered him a drink of water from the plastic bottle I had filled and treated for dysentery the night before. There were enough other hazards here without the risk of getting sick from dirty water. He drank deeply, returned the bottle with a smile, then stepped out onto the bridge.

For almost ten years Bob had been trying to get into this spot. He is a professional ornithologist, a scientist who studies birds, and when it comes to knowing South American birds he is about the best.

"We know a lot about the birds of Ecuador," he explained to me one day in his office at the Academy of Natural Sciences in Philadelphia, "except for one or two places where no one has ever been." He was pointing to the area marked *Cordillera de Cutucu* on the map in front of us. "Someday I'd like to explore those mountains and see what's in them."

That someday had finally come, and now, after years of planning, he was eager to get on with it. So was I. As a journalist and photographer, I had been invited to join the expedition so that I could report what entering unexplored land was really like. I was going to get more of a story than any of us bargained for.

We had started the expedition more than a week before in Quito, Ecuador's capital city far to the north. There we had met with government officials to finalize plans for exploring the Cutucu.

"We don't recommend entering Jívaro lands," warned one official. "The Jívaro, or Shuar, as they prefer to call themselves, are the most warlike of all Ec-

4

When Skip Glenn (right rear) and the author began to collect grasshoppers in Logroño, they were surrounded by children eager to give a hand.

uador's Indians. Even the Spanish could not conquer them." The warning was familiar to us. Many people had told us the same thing.

"We don't want to conquer them," explained Bob. "We just want to pass peacefully through their territory to study the birds that live there."

"Yes, I understand," said the official, "but I'm not sure they will believe it. You have our permission, but you'll have to get theirs. The Indians call the shots in the Cutucu."

With government approval and most of our provisions in hand, we had loaded a bus and driven south. The wide modern highway that led from the capital soon narrowed to a single lane. It turned and twisted and climbed into the high Andes, then dropped and climbed again.

Children came from far and wide to watch the scientists prepare for the Cutucu trek. Here, Dr. Frank Gill prepares bird specimens.

Two days and two nights later, we were in the frontier town of Logroño. The misty mounds of the Cutucu loomed beyond. From here we would have to travel on foot.

We made Logroño our base of operations for several days while we purchased more food, organized equipment, and arranged to hire Indian porters, mules, horses, and men to handle them. When not packing our gear or negotiating prices for various goods and services, we were catching insects nearby. With the help of children from a local school, we scoured Logroño's central square for grasshoppers.

The next morning the same children and their parents gathered to watch us pack our hundreds of pounds of supplies and march slowly out of town. For a while some of the younger children followed along, caught up by the excitement of our departure. The rest stood by the side of the road talking quietly among themselves. "Cutucu" and "Jívaro" were the words I heard the most. They were said with a disturbing hush, but it was too late for second thoughts now. After months of preparation, it felt good to be heading off at last.

I watched Bob bounce up and down on the swinging bridge as he crossed the Upano River border. The sound of his footsteps was lost to the steady drone of the river, whose roiled surface danced and glittered in the sunlight.

There were ten of us in all, not counting the mule drivers and Indian porters. Bob and I waited for the others in the shade of a banyan tree on the Indian side of the river. One by one they joined us at the far end of the bridge. Like us, each man carried a backpack filled with clothes and critical supplies. Like Bob, several carried guns and ammunition.

Behind them came the mules and horses, so heavily loaded with equipment that they were dwarfed by their bulky packs. They carried duffel bags, tents, blankets, sleeping bags, canvas sacks of rice and beans, pots, pans, jugs for water, tables, chairs, cans of food, lanterns, jars, nets, axes, and a hundred and one other bits of equipment that would be needed in the months ahead.

Drivers coaxed the six frightened animals onto the bridge, where they followed each other slowly, their hoofs slipping on the narrow wooden slats that held them above the rushing water.

From the end of the bridge, footpaths led in three directions. Two ran north and south along the river. The third pointed east toward the mountains. This was the trail we would follow.

At first the trail was wide and dry, passing through fields of towering reeds that grew so thick and high it was impossible to see anything beyond them. It was

The day of departure: Horses, mules, and porters gathered in the town square to prepare for the difficult trip ahead. Hundreds of pounds of food are loaded on the waiting animals.

easy walking and not at all the "impassable path" we had been warned to expect. But as we moved farther and farther from the river, the path began to narrow and deepen. The grassy fields gave way to heavier vegetation, then jungle trees that pushed at the edges of the trail, forcing us into single file. Within a few miles, the path had become a dark green tunnel that climbed and twisted like a leafy whirlpool, sucking us deeper and deeper into the Cutucu.

The air of the forest was damp and heavy, carrying with its heat the slight sweetness of decaying fruit. The trail grew softer as we climbed; it turned, at last, into a trench of slimy goo. Leaving the solid ground of the valley, we pushed on through oozing yellowish mud that clung to our legs like peanut butter, slowing our progress to an agonizing crawl.

We had trouble staying upright in the mud. So did the horses. Time and again, they lost their footing on the slippery rocks that underlay the trail. Sometimes, if the path was especially steep and narrow where they fell, they rolled back down it like misthrown bowling balls, scattering us to the sides and grinding the canvas packs of food and clothing into the mud. All up and down the trail we could hear the heavy slogging of their hooves and the shouts of the drivers urging them on, then more footsteps or the sickening crash of a falling animal.

The mules were tougher than the horses. They seemed stronger and steadier on their feet. When they fell, they got up again. The horses weren't so able.

"This fellow has carried his last load," said Francisco, one of the Indians who had agreed to help us as a guide and porter. He was standing over the largest of the packhorses, now lying in the trail. Broken branches and a long, smooth section of mud on the ground above told the story. The animal had fallen badly, rolling three or four times his length and lodging between a tree trunk and a rock. He was breathing noisily and could not get up.

"What can we do for him?" I asked.

Francisco shook his head. "Nothing," he answered. "The horse is done."

The Indian slipped a well-used hunting knife from a sheath on his belt and slowly cut the cords that held the animal's load. One of two large sacks of rice, torn in the horse's fall, spilled cream-colored grains into the mud.

"What will happen now?" I asked.

"We will take the rice," he said, without really answering my question.

"And the horse?" I continued.

"El Tigre will take the horse," he answered, looking up slowly from the panting animal to the jungle. I knew that El Tigre was the Indian's name for the jaguar. Unless the horse could rouse itself and follow our team to the safety of camp, it had little chance of living out the night.

A deep roll of thunder drew my thoughts back to the present. We had many miles to go before nightfall, and the trail was growing steeper by the yard. Nothing could be gained by staying there.

The rain came gently at first, then harder, spattering on the trail and soaking our heads and shoulders. We were spread apart now, traveling in two and threes or sometimes alone, along the same narrow thread of trail. The mules and horses had dropped behind.

"There's no way of getting lost," said Francisco as he doubled back to check on the lagging pack animals. "All the trails lead to the same place."

The instructions seemed reassuring at first, but as the trail divided, then split again, his words came back to me like looking-glass logic from *Alice in Wonderland*. How can all the trails lead to the same place when they go in different directions? I wondered. But there was no one to ask.

Hours later, as the dark of evening began to creep across the forest floor, many of us were still lost in the confusing spiderweb of trails. Unless we could find each other and a protected place to spend the night, El Tigre might have more to feed on than our abandoned horse.

"Let's fire a signal shot," suggested Bob Ridgely as the light began to fade. Bob, Mark Robbins, and I had caught up with each other at a stream crossing earlier in the afternoon and had been traveling together ever since.

In moving from one campsite to another, the author and each member of the expedition carried his own equipment.

"Good idea," said Mark, easing the leather strap of his shotgun over his shoulder and sliding a green plastic shell into the barrel. "We have five shotguns among us. Maybe someone will hear us and answer back."

At first there was only the deep far-off sound of a fast and noisy river, but then came the faint report of an answering gun. Its echoing boom, confirmed by a second exchange of fire, drew us on through muddy trails we could no longer see, with renewed hope and an energy level not felt since morning.

As the river grew louder and the blanketing vegetation gave way to starlight, we emerged into a large clearing. At its center, the metal roof of a small cabin shimmered in moon-washed twilight. Two figures stood by the cabin, gazing into the deep valley beyond. They looked small and fragile against the mountains, their silhouettes partly hidden by the knee-deep grass. Frank Gill, co-leader of the expedition, and Skip Glenn, another member of the team, turned and echoed our shouts of greeting. Later, inside the cabin, we talked excitedly of the day's experiences while we waited for the rest of the team.

Miraculously, one by one, they appeared. By ten o'clock we were all together under the shiny metal roof. Francisco had been right. The trails did lead here. But where was *here*, I wondered, and how did he know?

Shafts of moonlight pierced the wooden walls of the cabin, striping the edges of the floor and washing our tightly packed body mounds with a blue-green haze. From the loft above came laughter and murmuring voices as Francisco and the other Indian porters discussed the horrors of our first day's trek.

Slowly conversation gave way to sleep, and the cabin filled with heavy, ragged breathing. Outside, far down the valley, a Spectacled Owl began to call. Its deep, repetitious hoot was just audible above the soothing roar of the river.

Z

A Grisly Relic

If there was any reason to know the time, you could set your watch by an equatorial sunrise. Summer and winter the twelve-hour days in Ecuador begin and end at six o'clock.

The sun was up but not yet past the ridgetop when we began to stir. There was no rush, for we would spend this day in camp. We could not proceed until a second team of pack animals arrived from Logroño.

I thought of them and their drivers crossing the Upano bridge and entering the slimy trail that lay between it and camp and was glad not to be with them. I wondered if they would find our fallen horse, or if it had met El Tigre in the dark.

Our own pack animals had passed the night grazing by the safety of the cabin. Later, after a good rest and feed, they would be loaded up and taken ahead to another campsite. We planned to wait by the cabin for the second team, then travel on the next day.

"I don't think we should spend another night here,"

An unexpected cabin provided shelter for the first night in the Cutucu. An Indian lean-to attached to its rear held an unwelcome surprise and ominous warning.

said Juan José Espinosa, whose first name we had shortened to J.J. He was the youngest member of our team, a student from Ecuador's capital city of Quito, where he also served on the staff of the natural science museum. J.J. didn't speak often, so when he said anything, we listened. "I have a funny feeling about this place," he continued, "as though we shouldn't be here."

"There doesn't seem to be an owner of this cabin," observed Frank.

"That's what I mean," said J.J. "Don't you think it's strange that here, in the middle of the jungle, is a well-built cabin with no one in it?"

"The very fact that there is a cabin here at all seems strange to me," said Paul Greenfield, slapping the wooden wall of the building. A wildlife artist born in the United States, Paul had lived in Ecuador for ten years. Though he had not been to this area before, he was familiar with Indian life in Ecuador. "Shuar buildings are usually made of woven palm leaves and other local materials," he continued. "Except for the lean-to attached to the side of the building, there's nothing about this cabin that looks Shuar to me."

The comforting smell of woodsmoke and coffee interrupted our discussion and drew us to the makeshift kitchen Francisco had created under the lean-to shelter. There, two large pots, one of bubbling oatmeal, one of rice, hung above a well-built fire.

"Please feed yourselves," he said in Spanish, handing us metal bowls.

"The Indians use their hands to eat," said Frank in a

Francisco kept pots of rice and oatmeal bubbling over an open fire.

16

whisper. "We'll have to find the spoons somewhere in the other packs."

As the morning mist burned off the valley and the vultures rode the air currents of the ridge, our team members headed off in different directions, some to collect grasshoppers and butterflies, some to look for new birds, some to wash in the river and sun-dry on the smooth streamside rocks. Before joining the others by the water, I sat for a while in the cabin doorway, examining its heavy sawn-wood construction. It looked like a pioneer's cabin from our own West. Perhaps it was the work of a white colonist trying to establish a toehold beyond the Indian frontier, I thought.

With one of the highest birthrates in the world, Ecuador's population explosion is quickly driving both white and Indian farmers into the few remaining wild areas of the country. So far, the Shuar have kept these mountains as their own, but the frontiers are under constant pressure. Someday, without Shuar protection, the Cutucu may become a part of the creeping slash-and-burn agricultural advance that has destroyed so much of the wild land of Ecuador.

Whoever built the cabin had put a lot of effort into it, that was clear. The lumber was probably cut from large trees on the spot, but the tin roof and nails had to be carried from Logroño. Who was this enterprising pioneer, I wondered, and where was he now?

A soft breeze blew woodsmoke through the cabin and carried with it snatches of conversation from the Indians gathered by the fire. Above them the palm leaves of the lean-to roof flapped gently, rustling as they lifted and fell from a woven branch frame.

Mark Robbins waits out a rainstorm in "scalplock cabin."
Guns were never far from hand.

19

A long dark wisp, more like a shadow than a leaf, was moving too. It hung just below the roofline, silently brushing the lean-to's corner post. At first I barely noticed it; then, even before I had asked myself what it was, I knew. I knew why J.J. had felt uneasy in the cabin, why there was no owner here to claim the building as his own. Tucked up under the eaves of the shelter and all but hidden by the matted palms was a human scalp lock. Its long black hair waved like a flag of warning in the morning air.

I wanted to know from where—and whom—it had come, how long it had been there, and what it meant, but as my eyes dropped down to catch Francisco watching me, I knew I could never ask. He looked away quickly, poking at the fire with a smoking stick.

This would have to be my secret—our secret—at least for a while. For the others to see this grisly relic at the outset of the trip might so discourage them as to jeopardize the expedition. I had come as an observer. Now was a good time for me to keep my observations to myself.

By lunchtime, our team had grown in numbers and supplies. The second pack train, arrived from Logroño, had unloaded their animals and settled in for a meal of rice and beans. But already unexpected problems had arisen.

The first group of porters were Indians, proud of their heritage and of the land they shared. The second group, hired in Logroño, were white colonists, or *colonos*, with whom the Indians had fought for years. The

Todd Miller ponders the future of the expedition. After only a day, his well-laid plans and arrangements had begun to unravel.

21

two groups refused to work together and would not share food or shelter.

"Indian food is dog food," grumbled one *colono*, spitting toward the fire. "We want our own cook, our own rice, our own place to sleep." The support team that had taken us weeks to assemble was dissolving after only a day of work. Without knowing it, we had stepped into a hatred that ran back to the days of the first Spanish conquistadors.

Todd Miller, a Peace Corps volunteer who had helped us arrange for porters from his post near the Cutucu, had come in with the second pack train. Exhausted by his trek from Logroño and discouraged by the squabbling between porters, he met with Frank and Bob to work out a solution.

"Let's keep the two groups away from each other as long as we can," suggested Bob. "Why not send the Indian team ahead to prepare our next camp? They can spend the night there while we stay here with the *colonos*."

"I'll go with the Indians," offered J.J., pleased by a chance to leave the cabin.

"Good idea," said Paul. "Steve and I will join you." His brother nodded in agreement.

Todd relayed the plan to the porters, first in the Indians' language, then in Spanish. I admired his command of the languages and wished I could speak them as well.

Together we watched the Indians pack their mules and file slowly out of camp. Before fading from view at the clearing's edge, Francisco turned back for a last cold look.

3

Birds in Our Web

We had come to the Cutucu to study birds, and Bob Ridgely could hardly wait to start. He had been watching them with binoculars ever since leaving Logroño, but to gather the kind of information he needed, this was clearly not enough.

"We need to weigh and measure these birds and to make detailed photographs of each one," he explained as we sat by the fire that evening. "As soon as we can establish a camp, we will break out the mist nets and get to work."

Days later, when we had hiked far enough and high enough into the mountains to start our collecting, Bob began the process with a lesson in how to string nets.

"Each net is forty feet long and ten feet high," he explained, pulling the carefully rolled black nylon mesh from a cotton bag. "The idea is to stretch it tightly between two poles in a narrow lane cut from the forest. If the net is properly strung, the birds moving through the undergrowth will not see it. You will be surprised

23

how many will fly into the net and become tangled. As long as we get them out within an hour, they will not be hurt in any way."

After walking a good distance from camp along an old Shuar hunting trail, he stopped and pointed to a rise in the ground beside the path.

"Do you see that ridge?" he asked. "Birds will have to fly up and over it. Let's put a net along the top."

Skip, Todd, and I moved from the trail into the thick vegetation, slashing our way with the machetes we had brought from camp.

"Try to cut as few of the plants as possible," Bob said. "A lot of disturbance near the net will warn the birds that something is wrong there. All we want is an alley forty feet long and two feet wide along the crest."

"It looks like a volleyball net that goes all the way to the ground," said Todd, when we had finished setting the first net.

More like a long black spiderweb, I thought, admiring the shadowy wall of nylon we had stretched along the ridge. The top and bottom of the net were taut. In between hung rows of tiny bags designed to catch and hold the birds. From only a few steps away, the net was all but invisible.

By lunchtime we had strung a baker's dozen, and already they were having an effect. As we returned to camp, we stopped at each of the thirteen nets we had erected. Some were already twitching with birds.

Bob identified each bird as he removed it from the net and gently placed it in a cotton bag. There was a

The author untangles a captive bird from an all but invisible mist net, a delicate procedure that can take up to twenty minutes.

Bob Ridgely (left) and Frank Gill, co-leaders of the expedition, examine captured birds so unusual that even these experienced ornithologists were amazed.

Spotted Barbtail, a Black-capped Antshrike, a Wedge-billed Woodcreeper, and a brilliant blue-green hummingbird he called a Napo Sabrewing. There were spadebills, puffbirds, leaf-tossers, and foliage-gleaners. The names were as colorful as the birds.

As we approached the net nearest to camp, we could hear the excited scolding and chattering of birds. The noise was coming from five little brown wrens, four of which had been caught in the invisible mesh. The fifth wren, which had somehow avoided capture, was hopping excitedly from bush to bush nearby. Together they were making a racket ten times their size.

"These are Sepia-brown Wrens," explained Bob. "They often travel in family groups and are very loyal to each other. The wren not caught is probably one of the two parents. I suspect it will follow the family wherever we take them."

26

Just as Bob had predicted, the little bird not netted watched us de-net the other four, then trailed along as we carried the chattering birds back to camp.

"Let's photograph the wrens first so we can get them back together," I suggested as I set the camera on its tripod.

"Good idea," Bob replied. "They're getting more noisy by the minute." He removed the first wren from the small cotton bag in which we had carried it to camp. Then, keeping a firm grip of its feet, he held the bird in front of the camera. When I flashed its picture, the little wren suddenly stopped its scolding and burst into a beautiful warbling song. Tom Schulenberg dashed to his tent for a tape recorder. By the time he returned the free wren was singing too.

"They always say, 'A bird in the hand is worth two in the bush,'" whispered Todd as the birds sang and the tape rolled. "I'd say the two are about equal in making good music."

After we had photographed and measured each of the four wrens, we readied the birds for release by clipping the corners of their tails with a pair of scissors. Within a few months the wrens would molt the clipped feathers and grow new ones in their place, but for the time we would be there, this painless marking would help us tell which birds we had already examined and which we had not. If any of these birds were caught again, we would be able to recognize it.

"For many years the only way to study birds was to shoot them," said Bob as he held a bright blue bird he called a manakin for my camera. "All that changed after World War II when the first mist nets were brought from Japan. Ornithologists have been dependent on them ever since." The nets, he explained, enable scientists to capture birds they might not ever see just by walking through the woods.

"Many areas that were studied earlier now need to be restudied using mist nets," he said, releasing the

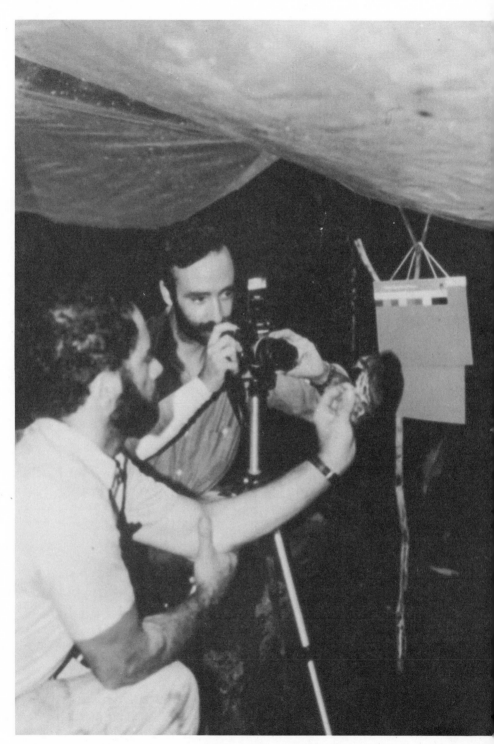

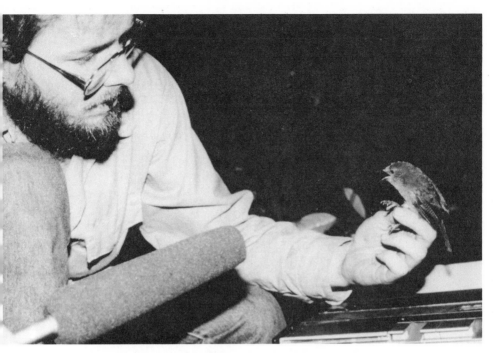

When held in the hand, this Sepia-brown Wren burst into a long warbling song. Tom Schulenberg recorded it for science.

When removed from the nets, each bird was brought to camp and photographed. Here Steve Greenfield holds one of the birds for the author.

manakin and pulling another bird from a holding bag nearby.

"This little fellow is an antpitta," he said, holding up a brown-and-white bird with large dark eyes. "It is very secretive and spends most of its life on the forest floor. If we hadn't caught him in a net, I doubt that we would ever have known he was here." I took several pictures as the bird blinked sleepily in the light.

"Unfortunately, mist nets won't get everything we need," Bob continued. "Some birds spend their whole lives in the forest canopy. We'll have to collect them the old-fashioned way."

Bob had been given special permission to shoot some of the birds we would find in this remote corner of Ecuador. As a conservationist, Bob was opposed to killing any wild species, but as a scientist, he knew that in order to gain an understanding of the little-known birds of the Cutucu, he would have to collect examples of each for anatomical study. Some of the birds he collected would be put in formaldehyde or alcohol for long-term preservation. Others would be skinned and their brilliant plumage used for comparison with closely related species already represented in museum collections.

The Collared Puffbird (facing page, top left) with its bright orange bill, white throat, and banded brown head, was caught early in the expedition. Its presence at about 6,000 feet elevation was unusual for this lowland forest dweller. The Chestnut-breasted Coronet (top right) a beautiful green, rufous, and bronze hummingbird about four inches in length, is found throughout the Cutucu and elsewhere in the Andes. The White-striped Warbler, bottom, was one of several rare birds photographed for the first time.

Mistrust between **colono** *muledrivers (left) and Indians (center) led to unexpected conflict almost from the start. Each accused the other of stealing food.*

33

For several years Bob had been working on a comprehensive book about the birds of all of South America. Once he had specimens from this unknown region, he could proceed with the important publication. I was excited to be a part of the final research for what promised to be a landmark book.

All afternoon team members shuttled in and out of camp, bringing newly caught birds from the nets. "I hope all of our days are as productive as this," Bob said as I snapped the last picture of the evening. Everything seemed to be going so well, it was hard to imagine that a few days earlier we had come close to giving up the expedition. After a week in the Cutucu, I was beginning to expect the unexpected.

Missing Food, Missing Men

"I don't see how we can go any farther," said Todd, shaking his head. "We can never carry all this food ourselves."

As we stood by the trailside, wondering what to do next, the mule drivers unlashed dozens of sacks of food and equipment from their weary animals and dumped them in a pile.

"The muleteers refuse to go on," Todd explained. "They say these trails are too difficult and dangerous for their animals. They are leaving our things here and returning to Logroño."

Since their first day in the Cutucu, the mule drivers had been unhappy with the steepness of the trails. The repeated falls of the mules and horses had finally convinced them to go back.

"We will have to make camp near here," said Frank Gill, after the last of the mules had gone. "We can carry the supplies there and then plan our next step."

"It will take us days to carry all this stuff," argued

Todd Miller (left), Frank Gill, and others reason with mule drivers on the verge of deserting. Without them, there would be no way to transport hundreds of pounds of food and equipment.

Todd. "There must be thousands of pounds of food."

"I wish there were," said Frank, "but I'm afraid we've lost some. Have you noticed that with each move there have been fewer packs? I think the mule drivers have been stealing food and hiding it in the jungle. No doubt they'll be picking it up on their way back to Logroño."

Despite the now-apparent losses, there were still many more supplies than we could carry. We would have to call back Francisco and the Indians, who had been sent ahead to cut a trail. Together with the remaining *colono* porters, they could ferry the muddy bags of food and equipment to a makeshift camp.

"I told you those men were worthless," complained Francisco when he learned of the muleteers' departure. "You cannot trust the *colonos*. Here you must count on the Shuar."

The campsite we established sat on high ground in the deep curve of a river. A large lean-to at its center

Expedition members Skip Glenn (left) and Paul Greenfield, carrying what food and equipment they can, prepare to move on to another camp.

Each campsite was carefully selected to provide ready access to fresh water and as much variety of habitat as possible.

Todd Miller's discovery of missing food brought the
Indian-colono conflict to a head.

and the blackened site of an old fire told us that we were not the first to use it.

"This is an old Shuar hunting camp," said Paul. "The Indians build such places to use when they are away from their villages. They'll not be pleased to find us here."

"How often do they visit these camps?" I asked.

"It's hard to say," he replied. "It depends on how often they go hunting and where they hope to find game. I would guess five or six times a year."

"Let's hope this isn't one of those times," I said.

By late afternoon the campsite was ablaze with colorful tents. Above them at the center stood the palm shelter of the Shuar, now covered with a fresh layer of waterproofing leaves. The Indians in our porter team would sleep there. The remaining *colonos* had made a separate shelter for themselves. Our tents spanned the distance in between. Around us flowed the river called Chiguaza, the sound of its rushing water mixing with the endless patter of rain.

"As I see it, we have three options left," said Frank that evening, as he placed a Coleman lantern at the center of the worktable. The rest of us arranged our seats in the crowded tent, our eyes adjusting to the brightness of the light.

"One, we can give up now, leave our equipment here, and go back to Logroño; two, we can make do with the few porters that are left and reduce the distance we travel; or, three, we can stay put for a while, send out for more porters, and see what happens."

"There's certainly plenty we can do here," said Mark. "I say let's stay in the mountains as long as we can." The rest of us agreed. There was no reason to leave. With a good camp and adequate food, we could stay for weeks.

"I'm worried about the porters," said Todd after some time. "The Indians and *colonos* aren't getting along at all. I see nothing but trouble ahead."

His prediction was born out within a day. The next morning, Todd found dozens of cans of tunafish missing from the work tent. His call of alarm brought the two porter factions to their worst confrontation of the trip. With raised voices and threats of violence, each accused the other of the theft. Hours later, when the shouting was over, the missing food was still nowhere to be seen and the *colonos* were ready to quit. For double the food and wages, they would consider going on. Without these, they refused to help us further.

"We will not work with savages," said one of the *colono* porters when Todd explained that we could pay them no more. "The Shuar are thieves and murderers, and we want nothing more to do with them. You may

41

do as you wish, but we are leaving." And so they did.

For days Francisco had promised that, given the chance, he could lure more reliable men from Shuar villages in the Amazon basin. Now was the time for him to try. With a handful of rice, a cooking pot, and a machete, he set off for the mission town of Yaupi, a two- to three-day hike from our streamside camp. How many men he could hire or whether he would return at all was anybody's guess.

"We'll give him a week," said Frank. "If he is not back by then, we'll have to think about heading home. In the meantime, let's make the most of where we are."

5

Setting a Trap

Within a few days we had settled into a steady routine of work. Most of it revolved around the mist nets and the birds they captured.

Since first erecting the nets, we had been careful to wrap them up, or "close" them, each evening, opening them again at dawn.

"Why can't we leave the nets open?" Todd asked late one afternoon as we folded the last of fifteen nets. "It would save a lot of time, and we might catch something in them we wouldn't see in the daytime."

"You're right," said Bob. "We would probably catch something, but I'm not sure you'd like to see what it is."

My curiosity was aroused. "Oh, come on," I pleaded. "Let's leave this one open. I'll take out whatever we catch."

"All right," agreed Bob. "We'll make an experiment, but remember, you asked for it."

As we walked back to camp, we passed Calixto, one

A Shuar palm-leaf shelter stood at the center of camp. This one slept up to ten men and was almost completely waterproof.

of the Indians who had been with us from the start. He was carrying one of the expedition's extra shotguns and a ball of string. Evidently Calixto was planning a nighttime experiment of his own. Todd and I followed along and watched as he carefully searched for game trails on the rocky slopes beside the river.

"He is looking for *wanta*," explained Todd. "It is a large rodent the size of a pig. If he can find a path it is fond of using, he will set a gun trap overnight. We may all eat wanta tomorrow."

When Calixto finally found the fresh trail he had been looking for, he cut two saplings with Y forks and drove them into the ground a few feet away. Into these he gently placed the gun, aiming it toward the place he expected the animal to walk that night. He tied one end of the string to a tree beyond the wanta trail, drew it across the path, and tied its other end to a small stick. Then, after loading the gun, he carefully drew back the hammer and propped the stick in place. The string ran tautly across the trail just a few inches above the ground. An animal (or anything else) walking along the narrow path could not help tripping the string and shooting itself.

"I can see why it's not good to walk in the woods at night," I said as the three of us headed back to camp together.

"Booby traps are only one of the dangers to avoid," said Todd. "Don't forget El Tigre."

"*Y todas las culebras*," added Calixto, reminding us of the many snakes of the tropics.

When the *colonos* were with us, one camp had been divided into three after dark. Now we had two centers of activity. The Indians sat by the fire talking, eating, and sometimes singing songs. We gringos gathered in the work tent and, when dinner was over, prepared bird and insect specimens by the light of the Coleman lantern.

That night Todd and I told the others of the mist net we had left open and of the gun trap Calixto had set by the riverbank.

"The Shuar usually do their hunting in the daytime with blowguns," explained Paul after he had heard our description of the wanta trap, "but they have learned to use all kinds of gadgets—even guns, when they can get them. They hate to be out at night—"

"—because of the snakes and jaguars," inserted Todd.

"Yes," said Paul, "and also because of the wild spirits they believe inhabit the forest. Anyway, they have long been masters of the art of booby-trapping. With traps they can catch the night animals they might never see otherwise."

"If you ever had to travel at night, it's wise to take a

The remaining Shuar porters give the author a few pointers on using a machete.

walking stick," said J.J., looking up from the table where he was skinning a small bird. "If you walk the trail tapping the ground ahead like a blind man, you might avoid being booby-trapped yourself." The advice sounded useful to remember.

As Paul and J.J. talked more about the Shuar, I became fascinated by the thought of a people so well adapted to their land. I wanted to hear more from the Indians themselves. Encouraged by Calixto's friendliness earlier in the evening, I decided that this would be a good night to begin a dialogue. When I suggested the idea to Todd, he agreed to help by serving as a translator. Together we left the well-lighted work tent and walked the short distance to the Indian fire. It was like walking back centuries in time.

Calixto, the oldest of the four Indians, sat closest to the glowing warmth of the fire. His face was a map of wrinkles, his eyes two beads of light within an eight-shaped pool of shadow. Beside him sat Gabriel, next in age but younger by a decade. He was the largest and strongest of the Indians, with broad shoulders and an open, friendly face. Gabriel wore only shorts, and the light of the fire played on his muscular chest and arms. The two other Indians, Angel and Donato, were also shirtless, and their wiry bodies spoke of much hard work. They were younger than the others—sixteen or seventeen years old—but more than able to carry the same size loads as the older men. Calixto wore a hat; the other three had thick black bowl-cut hair.

Without the help of the Shuar guides, we could never have made our way into the Cutucu. This was their land and they knew it well. Though we could not speak each other's language, we learned to communicate in other ways.

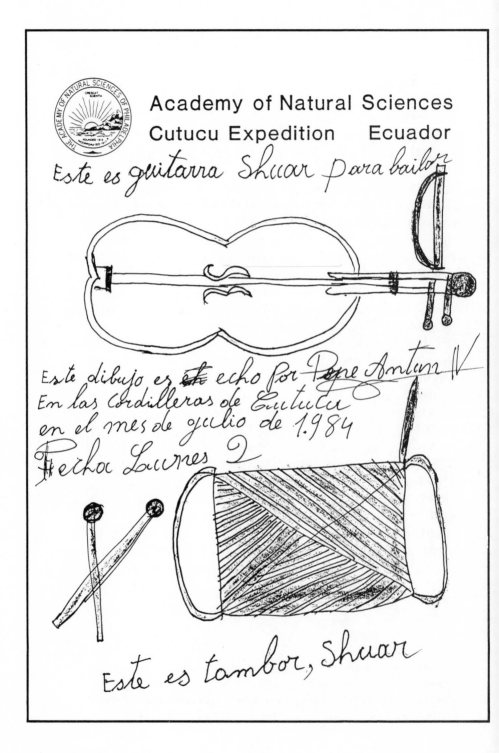

Academy of Natural Sciences
Cutucu Expedition   Ecuador

Este es guitarra Shuar para bailar

Este dibujo es ~~este~~ echo Por ~~Pepe~~ Antun V
En las Cordilleras de Cutucu
en el mes de julio de 1984
~~Fecha~~ Lunes 2

Este es tambor, Shuar

50

At first our conversation was rough and halting, with many gaps of silence. Calixto could speak Spanish, the other three only Shuar. The Indians were cautious, unwilling to open themselves to our questions. Then I brought out a box of crayons and several sheets of paper.

"See if they will draw pictures," I told Todd. "Ask Angel or Gabriel if he will draw his village for me." The idea intrigued them. Donato lighted a candle, and Gabriel began to draw.

It was the beginning of a series of such evenings, when, after dinner and daily chores were through, I joined the Indians in their shelter with pencil, crayons, and paper. Without benefit of language, they took me on a fascinating trip into their world. This night a lone hunter stalked El Tigre in the hills. The next, a village ceremony with dancers and instruments appeared. Pépé drew the instruments first: a flute, a drum, a two-stringed guitar. Next came the men and women who played them. Though he worked in silence, we could hear the music of celebration in his every line.

A different kind of music filled the air outside the shelter. Frogs croaked, chirped, and trilled from the darkness of the forest. Far up the mountain an owl called, then grew silent. I thought of the open mist net and wondered what might be tangled in its mesh. I remembered Calixto's gun trap and thought of the animals that could cross its path at any time.

Some of the Indians had a special talent for drawing. At the author's request, one sketched this Shuar guitar and drum on expedition stationery. Another later added the identifying captions.

51

That night, my dreams were filled with music, with Shuar villages and hunting trails, prowling animals, blowguns and traps. Twice I awoke, imagining a gunshot in the darkness, then faded back to sleep, soothed by the rush of the river and the muffled sound of raindrops on the tent.

The next time I awoke, it was with the sudden certainty that someone was standing by my tent. I sat upright, straining to hear more of the movement that had awakened me. There was no further sound. Suddenly with a single sweep the mosquito-netting zipper was undone. Through the open flap of the tent I could see two beady eyes and a shadowy figure. It was Calixto.

"Ven conmigo," he said. *"Es el momento de inspeccionar las trampas."*

I threw on my clothes and boots and stepped out into the predawn dampness. The rain had stopped, and there was a sliver of light on the eastern horizon, just visible through the heavy tangle of trees.

6
Monkey for Breakfast

We climbed up the hunting trail that led from camp, then left it for a game trail so small I could barely see it in the morning darkness. Calixto moved as quietly as the animals whose path we followed and so quickly I was hard-pressed to keep up. When he stopped, I almost bumped into him from behind.

In front of us, on the ground, lay the fallen string. The gun, its hammer down, was still in place, aimed at about knee height. The wanta had been there and tripped the cord, but the gun had failed to fire.

Calixto angrily picked up the gun and opened it. The shell had been hit but not ignited. Rusted slightly by the constant damp, the gun's hammer had not moved freely to the shell.

"The spirits have saved the wanta," said Calixto. "I will not set another trap here."

"It looks as if we're doomed to oatmeal," joked Bob at breakfast when I explained what had happened to the gun. "Unless, of course, you find something to eat in the open net." In the excitement of the morning I had almost forgotten our experiment.

"I'd stick to oatmeal if I were you," said Frank, who had checked the net while I was with Calixto. "There's always a chance of snagging an owl," he continued, "but unfortunately we didn't."

"The net is empty?" I asked with disappointment.

"Oh, no, you caught something, all right, but not an owl. You'll see. I left everything just as it was."

I hurried out of camp and along the trail to the net we had left open. Then I stopped as suddenly as Calixto had at the trap. The net was a writhing mass of dark, furry bodies. It was filled with rat-sized bats.

The mesh had been too fine for even the bats' delicate radar to detect. As they pursued insects on the wing, they had struck this unexpected obstacle and been caught. One look at their large teeth made clear the need for work gloves.

Just a year before, Bob Ridgely had been bitten by a bat while removing it from a net. Since the animal may have been carrying rabies, he had had to endure the long and painful series of shots devised to combat the disease. I wasn't going to take the same chance. I went back to camp for gloves, then returned to extract the writhing mammals.

After a long morning of work releasing the unwelcome captives one by one, I returned eagerly to my photographic duties in camp. I hadn't been there long before the quiet was broken by the wild whoops and

This drawing shows a Shuar hunter killing a monkey with a blowgun and poison dart, while another Indian paddles a dugout canoe below. The bird on the branch is probably the Chestnut-breasted Coronet, a hummingbird.

54

Academy of Natural Sciences
Cutucu Expedition   Ecuador

cordiyera del cutueu
Julio 3 del Año 1.984

cordiyera del cutueu
Julio 3 del Año 1.984

ehcanoa se va
un onvre

un honvre que sopla
la bodoKera
A mono

Carlos was a crack shot with his muzzle-loading musket. He kept his gunpowder and lead shot in a leather bag around his neck. Here he shows off a beautiful Masked Trogon before eating it for breakfast.

cries of half a dozen men running into camp. It was Francisco and a team of six new Indian porters from across the mountains. Within a few hours another group arrived to join them. From an inadequate four or five, our expedition's work force had grown to nineteen in a single day. We celebrated their arrival with an afternoon of feasting.

Among the new recruits was an Indian named Carlos, an energetic man of thirty who carried with him not the traditional Shuar blowgun but an ancient musket, salvaged perhaps from some long-forgotten expedition. As the only gun owned by any of the Indians, it gave Carlos special status.

Some days later, after Carlos had grown accustomed to my evening visits to the Indians' shelter, I asked him to show me his gun. It was almost as tall as I am and very heavy. It had a thick wooden stock, a long barrel, and, beneath it, an even longer metal ramrod. The gun's large hammer mechanism was of the percussion type, used in the United States at the time of the Civil War.

Unlike our modern guns that take shells from the breach, Carlos's musket was a muzzle-loader. To ready it for firing, he took his gunpowder flask, measured a charge of the loose black grains, poured them into the barrel, and packed them down with the ramrod. Next followed a measured mass of shot pellets the size of BBs. These too were packed. Finally he cocked the hammer and placed on the thin metal nipple below it a copper cap shaped like a tiny thimble. When struck, this would explode into the barrel, lighting the powder and setting off the gun with a deep, throaty bang and a huge cloud of smelly gray smoke.

Carlos was not happy with the gunpowder he was using. He complained that it was of poor quality and often misfired because of the constant dampness of the jungle. Each morning before leaving camp he tried to dry the powder by heating it in a frying pan over the open flame of the fire. The other Indians had total faith in his steady hand, but I knew what a terrible explosion could occur if the powder got too hot. I tried to stay a good distance away.

One afternoon Carlos asked Todd for permission to take his gun into the jungle in search of food. Our supplies were running low, he argued, and fresh meat would help to boost camp morale.

Since leaving our Chiguaza River camp, we had not seen any game animals. We knew Carlos would have to travel a good distance to find any, and we were reluctant to let him go. In the end, it was Paul's advice we heeded.

"If he goes hunting and finds nothing to shoot, he will blame the spirits for bad luck," Paul argued. "If we try to stop him from hunting, he will blame us. In order to keep the porter crew happy, I think we should let him go." Reluctantly, we agreed.

Carlos, with four other men, left camp in high spirits. By nightfall they were back with game, but not what we had expected. Draped over Carlos's shoulders like a winter scarf were the bodies of two black woolly monkeys. One of the Indians with him carried a third.

"*Mono*," Carlos announced triumphantly.

Carlos and the Indians who had been with him talked and laughed by the fire long into the night. With their voices came the forgotten smell of cooking meat. By breakfast the next morning, we were ravenous, looking forward to sharing the spoils of the hunt. But when Pépé, the cook, brought our meal, it was the usual pot of runny oatmeal. The Indians had been eating the monkeys through the night. Very little remained, and this they were reluctant to share. Finally, at Todd's insistence, the last bit of monkey meat was brought to our work tent. It was a plate of hands and feet.

Cordillera is the Spanish word for mountain chain, and *cutucu* the Shuar Indian word for moss. As we moved higher and higher into the mountains, we understood how and why the Cordillera de Cutucu had been so named. Every tree trunk and branch was covered with a soft, spongy moss that could hold five times its weight in water. And water, it seemed, was everywhere. At a camp the Indians named Yapitya we found

In this Indian illustration, the Shuar hunter carries a blowgun, a knife, and a quiver of poison darts. A large, spotted jaguar (with whiskers, pointed ears, and a long tail) lurks behind a giant palm. Note the bare feet of the hunter and the unusual perspective of his arms.

Academy of Natural Sciences
Cutucu Expedition   Ecuador

59

The Cutucu Expedition team. From left to right: Frank Gill (co-leader), Paul Greenfield, Skip Glenn, Todd Miller, Bob Ridgely (co-leader), Juan José Espinosa (sitting on stump), Mark Robbins, Tom Schulenberg, Steve Greenfield, and the author.

that, despite protection from above, the floors of our tents filled up like water balloons.

A month of almost steady rain was beginning to have its effects on clothing and equipment. Shirts were rotting, leather shoes, belts, and pack patches were turning green with mold, and most of our electrical gadgets, from tape recorder to camera flash, had long since failed to function. Our camps were tented cities, where huge plastic tarps sheltered us from rainfall but not from the moisture in the air. Clothes hung out to dry absorbed more water than they shed. Our rice was molding, open cuts refused to heal. But despite the soggy weather, spirits in camp remained remarkably high. There had been no serious illnesses or injuries, and our work was successful beyond our hopes.

The time had come for half of our team to return to Logroño and the modern world beyond. Bob Ridgely, Frank Gill, and the Greenfield brothers, Paul and Steve, had commitments in the United States. J.J. had to get back to Quito for a series of final exams. Mark, Tom, Skip, Todd, and I would stay to complete the work with ten of the original porter team. Five of these, led by Carlos, would accompany the departing members to Logroño, returning in a week with extra food supplies. The rest, under Francisco's direction, would begin the long process of clearing a trail from Yapitya camp to another campsite farther up the mountain.

For several weeks there had been a growing tension between Carlos and Francisco. We were pleased that, for a week at least, the two would be apart.

Juan Jose ("J.J.") Espinosa, of Ecuador's Natural History Museum, kept spirits high despite the hardships of the expedition.

No sooner had Carlos gone than Francisco began to complain about him. "The gun Indian is a bad Indian," Francisco advised. "He has been the cause of many problems. He is not to be trusted."

Days later, when Carlos returned from Logroño, he brought a note from Frank and Bob that told a different story.

"Look out for Francisco," it warned. "He is not what he seems. Our porters tell us that he has killed a woman in Yaupi, and maybe men as well. They suspect he and Calixto are stealing supplies. Do what you can to stop them, but be careful."

The others stood in silence as I read the note aloud.

"There is a P.S.," I said, turning to a smudgy scribble on the back of the sheet. " 'Sacrifice food if you must,' it says, 'but for God's sake, hold on to the guns.' "

"Keep talking, but change the subject," whispered Mark. "We have a visitor."

"We're having a lovely time in Logroño," I stammered, pretending to read the letter, but making up words as I went along. "The weather's great, wish you were here—"

Calixto was standing behind me. "*Quiero una escopeta,*" he cut in, pointing to one of our shotguns. "*Quiero hacer una trampa para wantas.*"

"Not today," said Todd quickly, picking up the gun and slinging it over his shoulder. "*Hoy día no.* We're going on a hunting trip and we need all the guns ourselves."

Mark and Skip moved slowly between Calixto and the work tent, where the other guns were stored. Calixto eyed us. "*Escopeta,*" he said again, repeating the Spanish word for shotgun.

"Sorry," said Todd firmly, "*escopetas no.*"

7

Terror on the Trail

By the following day, camp life seemed to have returned to normal. We tried to keep Francisco and Calixto busy and away from the center of activity by having them lead an Indian work crew in cutting a trail to our next campsite. In the meantime, Carlos helped us with camp chores and stringing new nets.

The passing of a morning storm promised clear weather for the afternoon. It seemed a good time for me to climb to the top of the ridge nearest our camp. From there I hoped to see at least some part of where we had been and where we were going in the Cutucu. With a tripod in hand and a daypack filled with camera equipment on my back, I set off shortly after lunch. Carlos had shown me the narrow Shuar hunting trail that would take me up the ridge. A cut twig, a turned log, or rearranged branch were all that showed the way. Otherwise, the trace was invisible.

Brilliant blue morphos and other butterflies with transparent wings fluttered near pools of light on the forest floor. Moisture dripped from the canopy above and rose from the leaf litter. It filled the air with the warm smells of earth and tiny droplets of water that caught the light in long shafts of silver and gold. Hummingbirds darted between flowering trees, sipping at the nectar of the waxy blossoms, then buzzing out of sight.

The trail climbed and twisted between moss-covered tree trunks as thick as train cars. Strangler figs wreathing the upper branches of the trees dropped long vine-like roots to the ground. Orchids and bromeliads, clinging to the trunks and branches, brightened the emerald green of the forest with red, yellow, and white blooms.

More than once, distracted by a bird, insect, or bright flower, I wandered off the trail and became lost within only a few yards of its safety. Each time, by crossing back and forth, I was able to regain my bearings and continue.

As the trail climbed higher on the ridge, the vegetation became lower, denser, and wetter. Dwarf trees with interlocking branches made tunnels of moss. Water droplets glistened in the sunlight. Birds scolded invisibly from the heavy growth. The ground, a network of woven roots, concealed dark caverns of various sizes. This was the first "elfin forest" I had ever seen. It was as mysterious and magical as its name suggests. I had entered an enchanted place well suited to elves and hobbits, but not fit for me. Though I placed each footstep with care, every few yards I found my-

Without maps to guide us, we hacked our way from ridgetop to ridgetop, leaving a narrow muddy trail. Between rainstorms, the mists would clear to reveal the mountains beyond.

self breaking through and into the subterranean caverns the roots concealed.

Mud-covered and dripping with water, I climbed back out into the sunlight and pushed on. In time, the full-grown trees stood no taller than my head. The trail grew more and more steep, then suddenly leveled off and turned into a clearing with an uninterrupted view eastward toward the Amazon.

Ridges piled one atop the next, some shrouded in mist, others fully revealed by the brilliance of the late-afternoon sun. Sounds of birds, frogs, and insects, carried on unseen winds, drifted up from the valley. There were other sounds too: the steady hiss of an unseen stream, and the occasional crash of an ancient tree grown top-heavy with parasitic vines. This was one of the last great rain forests unspoiled by man. It stretched north and south as far as my eye could travel.

Another few hundred yards up the trail, the sharp zigzag of the ridge brought me to another overlook. This time the view was to the west, where the sun was dropping behind the snow-capped peaks of the Andes.

It had been just under two hours to make the climb to the top. In order to reach camp by sundown, I would have to leave shortly. I set up the tripod and camera and began to photograph the valley, looking across the Upano River, north and west toward Logroño.

Though the sky was mostly free of clouds, the Cutucu seemed to be making rainy weather of its own. Between thick banks of moisture that swept up the ridge, I snapped photographs. For several minutes at a time I was unable to see beyond the tiny patch of ground on which I was standing. Then the cloud would pass and I could see to the far horizon.

After several mists had come and gone, I moved back to the first overlook to photograph the eastern Cutucu. Long shafts of afternoon sun bathed the slopes across

This ridgetop view almost cost the author his life.

the valley in a warm yellow light. From my ridge the treetops looked soft and even, like the surface of a rough green sponge.

I was already pushing my time limits to the edge of safety. To have sufficient light to reach camp, I knew it was time to leave, but somehow I could not. Despite weeks in the Cutucu, I had not, until now, had a really clear view of their vastness. The view, like the elfin forest, was strangely mesmerizing, and I was reluctant to leave. As the sun sank more deeply behind the jagged Andean peaks, its light grew strangely warmer and more intense. I snapped more photographs. From nowhere a cloud moved over me, chilling the air and coating everything with a thin layer of moisture. Then, as suddenly, it moved away and more ridges were revealed.

Seen from a distance, the Cordillera de Cutucu looks gently sloping. Seen closer at hand, they are an endless series of steep ridges covered with an all but impenetrable rain forest.

When the sun sets at the equator, it goes down quickly. There is little time for lingering twilight. I knew I had only half an hour to find my way back down the narrow path. It was less than a third the time needed for the trip. I had no sweater or jacket, no food, no flashlight, not even a match. Only speed and good luck would see me home.

I folded my tripod and stowed my camera gear, then paused for one final look at the great wilderness that stretched out before me. Such visions are rare in the world today. They can make a person feel small and vulnerable. The view was awe-inspiring and, together with a closing mist, sent a shiver down my back. I was an intruder here. It was time to leave.

To go as far as I could with what light was left, I began running almost at once, ducking under the low branches of the elfin forest, leaping from root to root across the matted ground, slipping, falling, breaking through the concealing surface, then emerging from the sodden darkness and rushing on.

Once past the elfin forest, the trail grew steeper and more slippery, speeding my travel but increasing the frequency of my falls. The light was fading quickly now. I was afraid of missing the trail and losing my way in the darkening forest. I also knew that this was the time for jaguars and snakes to make their appearance on the trail. With each unexplained sound or hint of movement in the forest, I quickened my pace.

As the trail grew steeper, I could cover four to six feet with a single step, catching my weight on a rock or root, breaking my falls by grabbing the trunks and branches of the flanking forest. Faster and faster I went, passing in minutes sections of trail that had taken three times as long to climb.

I had just picked myself up from a tumble and regained my speed. Then, in a horrifying second, I knew that something was terribly wrong. A large "root" on which I was about to catch my weight was moving.

A person's eyes can play strange tricks in the tropical twilight, but this was not a time for second glances—or second chances. Stretched its full length across the trail lay a giant snake. Its head and tail were hidden by the undergrowth at either side. Only a foot of its patchy brown and black skin was visible.

If I were traveling through lowland rain forest, this briefly glimpsed creature could have been any one of several species. But here, at a higher elevation, it most likely was the worst—the deadly bushmaster. Among the most feared of poisonous snakes, the bushmaster has a bite that is almost always fatal. A single drop of its venom can kill a child. A direct, double-fanged strike can kill a cow.

These thoughts raced through my mind as my body flew through the air. It was too late to redirect. The only hope now was to pass before the snake could strike. My left foot landed squarely in the center of its back. Like a dream, everything moved in slow motion as I bounded on. A warm dizzying rush of blood flowed through my body. Heavy breathing and the throbbing of my heart were the only sounds I could hear.

The rest of my trip down the mountain is now a blur of memory, more dream than reality, for the adrenaline that rushed through my veins, giving me new speed and energy, had also numbed my senses. My feet barely seemed to touch the ground. When I fell, as I must have done often, I felt nothing, rolling, somersaulting, and getting up again to race on in the growing darkness. If you have ever had a dream of flying, you have felt the way I felt that night. Not until I reached camp did I pause for rest.

Never were the sound of voices and the glow of lamplight more welcome. The tiny beacon of light that came from the work-tent door drew me from the darkness like a moth.

Mark, Tom, Skip, and Todd had long since finished dinner and were at work preparing bird skins by the light of the Coleman lantern. I stood for a while, listening to their voices and gasping for breath, before unzipping the tent door. I was shaking when I finally went inside.

"Good God! What happened to you?" asked Mark when he saw me at the door. The others stared at me almost without recognition.

"You look like you've been through a war," said

This Shuar drawing of a giant snake was an uncanny foreshadowing of the bushmaster the author was to meet on the trail.

 **Academy of Natural Sciences**
Cutucu Expedition   Ecuador

Sr Dón Marco Unitiveh

73

Todd, and indeed I did. My face and body were cut and bruised, my clothes torn and muddy.

"Another ten minutes, and we were going to come looking for you," said Mark.

"Another ten minutes and I might never have come back at all," I replied. Then I began to tell the story of my long mountain run. If I had left the top of the ridge ten minutes later, I would never have found the trail. Had I been any later than I was, I would have had to slow my descent, groping for footholds with my toes. I would have found the snake, not with my eyes but through the sharp strike of its deadly fangs.

Death Threat

The excitement of my ridgetop adventure soon faded in the routine of camp life. There were nets to open, check, and close, new birds to photograph, insects to catch and prepare, and a daily journal to keep up-to-date.

Tensions among the porters continued to build. Then one day Francisco pulled Todd aside. He announced that he and Calixto would refuse to do the work required unless they were paid twice the rate of the other porters. When Todd brought us the news, we saw the chance we had been looking for to get rid of Francisco's threatening presence. If we refused to meet their demands, Francisco and Calixto would have no choice but to leave or to lose face among the porters.

"There is one other possibility," warned Todd as we discussed the best course of action. "Don't forget, Francisco has already killed a person. What's to keep him from killing again?"

"These," said Mark, pointing to the guns. "You and

75

I will give him the message; the rest can back us up."

Though the two Indians had made me uneasy, I was sorry to see them leave. Both had been with us from the start. Calixto's feel for animals and skill at setting traps had intrigued me. Francisco was equally adept at building shelters. Perhaps they felt my admiration, for, unexpectedly, they sought me out to say goodbye. I took a last picture of them as they headed off down the trail.

Hours later, Skip and I encountered them again, only a short distance from camp. This time they were traveling in the other direction and carrying two large canvas sacks. They seemed surprised to see us. Then, after a moment's hestitation, they put down their bags and rushed up to shake our hands. Evenly matched in number, we thought better of asking them about their newly acquired luggage. We simply smiled and returned their greeting, then watched in silence as they picked up their sacks, turned, and disappeared into the forest. We never saw them again.

One evening a few days later, when Todd and I returned to camp from a last net check, we found the place astir. A young dark-skinned Indian with a heavily tattooed face was squatting by the fire. Pépé, our camp cook, and Marco, his helper, were beside him, pumping him with questions in the musical dialect distinctive of the Shuar. All three jumped up when we arrived. The rest of the camp was empty.

Todd put down the bird bags he was carrying and tried to greet the newcomer with a handshake, but the man backed away in silence. His eyes darted be-

The author makes notes during a rare break in the rain. Special waterproof paper and ink helped field journals survive.

tween us, his hands fidgeting with a sheathless machete. Todd backed off too, then gestured to the rice pot, inviting the Indian to share our food and shelter.

By the time the others returned for dinner, the new arrival had made himself at home among the porters. His voice, higher and more nasal then the rest, drifted from their fireside shelter through the evening, muffled, at times, by the drumming of an all-night rain.

"With Francisco and Calixto gone, it might be a good idea to hire this Indian as an extra porter," I suggested as we prepared for bed. The others agreed.

The next morning Todd joined the Indians over breakfast to extend our invitation. He came back so pale I thought he was sick.

"What's wrong? What did he say?" asked Mark as the rest of us gathered around.

"Is it the porters?" we asked. "What do they want?"

"It isn't the porters," he answered at last, "It's the Shuar . . . and they want us."

Through garbled translation, Todd had learned that the Shuar leaders no longer believed that we were birdwatching. They thought it more likely that we were looking for gold and other valuables. Knowing that such resource discoveries could lead to exploitation of the Cutucu and a loss of their own control, they had ordered it stopped.

"We are to be attacked and killed or driven from the mountains," reported Todd. "Whoever does the job will be rewarded with our equipment and remaining food."

For several minutes the five of us stood in silence, absorbing Todd's message and wondering how things could have gone so wrong. Long before we set out on

As food supplies dwindled, patience grew thin among the Indian porters. Team members wondered which ones could be counted on when the chips were down.

Frank Gill, Skip Glenn, and Tom Schulenberg force down a meal of moldy noodles and bird bodies, mixed in a peanut-butter sauce. (Later in the trip, meals would get smaller and much worse.)

the expedition, Todd had sought permission for us to enter these mountains. The Ecuadoran government had said we could make the trip if the idea was approved by the Shuar representatives in Sucúa. After months of consideration, an Indian spokesman there had said it would be all right. Unfortunately, as we had now learned the hard way, loosely organized political federations rarely speak with a single voice. For whatever reason, their promise of safe passage had been reversed.

"I've been in trouble before," said Todd, "but never like this!" Our nervous laughter echoed his.

"But how do we know this is true?" asked Tom.

"Everyone seems to know it," said Todd. "Everyone but us."

For all their primitive ways, the Shuar are sophisticated at communicating among themselves. The hit order, an instruction as old as the tribe itself, was broadcast by shortwave radio from Shuar headquarters in Sucúa to the handful of Indians who own receivers. From there the word had been carried by mouth. According to our visitor, our unwelcome status in the mountains was now general knowledge among the tribe.

Perhaps the young warrior had come to warn his friends . . . or to ask for their help. Maybe he was in camp to see for himself the value of the equipment that had been offered as reward for our death. Whatever his motives, he did not stay long. By midmorning he was gone, and with him two of the ten porters.

Tom seemed unaffected by the news and eager to get on with the work at hand. "There's nothing to be gained by sitting around here," he said, slinging a shotgun over his shoulder and walking out of camp. The rest of us took shotguns too, then gathered in the work tent to decide our next course of action. The remaining Indians busied themselves in camp. They seemed to have decided to stick it out with us—at least for a while.

To return to Logroño now would mean following known trails, camping at known campsites, and passing close to the very Shuar villages we would most like to avoid. Staying where we were seemed equally risky and was of little appeal to the birders, who had been working this area for over a week. The third option, going deeper into the Cutucu, farther away from Shuar settlements, would at least buy time, though not a great deal. Todd estimated that only two weeks' worth of food remained.

Given the alternatives, two weeks seemed better than none, and new territory more appealing than old. The decision was unanimous. The next day we would break camp and move five or six miles to a new site. Like our last three moves, it would be an all-day trek on trails our porters had been cutting for days.

An Indian guide displays a stringer of rocksuckers. The rubbery lips were later eaten in a slimy gray soup.

There had been so many problems on this trip, the death threat simply joined the list. In this surreal world of brilliant birds and moss-draped jungle, the idea seemed more fantasy than fact. More pressing were the daily needs of food and sleep.

Of these, food was the most urgent. It was now too far and too dangerous to send porters back for more supplies. We would have to make do with what we had and stretch this by what we could find to eat in the mountains.

Our lunch was a sample of the horrible meals to follow. In a burst of misguided creativity, our cook served moldy noodles covered with a sickening sauce of asparagus soup and peanut butter. It was all we could do to force it down. In the days ahead we would grow used to eating the broiled bodies of the tiny birds we caught to skin.

The Indian porters were more resourceful at finding local food. From decaying logs and stumps, they unearthed sausage-sized wood grubs. They considered these wiggling maggots great delicacies. They also enjoyed eating the armored catfish that lived in the mountain streams near camp. These scaly fish normally spend their lives sucking on the slime-covered rocks of the river bottom. When time would permit, the Indians caught them by hand, peeled them from the rocks, and boiled them into a thick, gelatinous soup. We soon learned that the fish themselves had far too many bones for eating, but the large, rubbery lips could be peeled off and eaten separately.

"Who would have ever guessed a bowl of rice and rock-sucker lips would be the highlight of a day?" joked Todd over our evening meal.

"We may look back on these as the good old days when we still had food," answered Mark with a smile. "Please pass the pepper."

9

Tarantula!

After a long morning of felling tents, packing equipment, and preparing for our trek farther into the mountains, we left Yapitya camp and strung out single file along the narrow trail that had been cut for us. It led up and down through forest so thick we could not see more than a few dozen yards to either side. Troops of woolly monkeys, disturbed by our passing, leaped through the treetops, chattering noisily. A covey of Rufous-breasted Wood Quail exploded from the leafy ground ahead. Other birds and animals, less easily seen, rustled off through the forest as we passed.

We traveled in twos or threes, gathering at river crossings, then spreading out again according to each person's strength and speed. Our heavy packs, guns, and camping gear slowed each mile to an agonizing crawl.

By midafternoon we reached a trail section even more narrow than the rest. The ground dropped steeply to

right and left, leaving a walking surface just wide
enough to support a single file. Although the trail had
been cut for our use within the past few days, the signs
of its recent clearing were already disappearing. Fun-
gus and mold had covered some of the jagged stumps,
and the many severed branches that lined the trail had
already dropped their leaves and so begun the rapid
process of decay. Life and death moved quickly in the
tropics. Within six months our trail would be re-
claimed by the forest, invisible to all but the keenest
eyes.

"I'm glad we don't have to camp here," I called to

Heavy packs, stiff currents, and slippery rocks made each river crossing a hazard.

Todd as I followed him along the ridge. "There's not a level surface anywhere."

"Someone else has found a way to do it," he answered a few minutes later. We both stopped and stared wide-eyed at the trail ahead. There, at its very center, was a freshly built shelter made of palms.

"Shuar!" we whispered together.

The lean-to stood no more than four feet tall, a central post with several dozen palm boughs rising tent-like to its top. We had seen them before, in the lowland forests closer to the border. This one- or two-man shelter had been built and used within the last twenty-four hours. It was empty now, except for the leaves spread on the ground inside. We edged carefully around it and continued on our way, silent and more cautious. Each member of the expedition would encounter the structure in turn. Each would pass it with the knowledge that we were not alone.

Our own campsite, some miles farther on, had not yet been cleared when we arrived. Though wider than the trail ridge and off to one side, the area was not as broad or as level as we would have liked. Our work and sleeping tents would take every inch of available space. At this camp, like the others, we could expect almost continuous rain. Good tarpaulin covers would be important, and there were only a few large trees from which to stretch them.

"I don't like the looks of this site," said Mark, wading through chest-high brush, "but we haven't much choice. The rest of the ridge is too narrow and we're running out of time." It was just past five thirty, leaving less than half an hour of light for us to clear the site and pitch our tents. "Let's get to work."

At Carlos's direction, the porters left their packs by the trail and fanned out through the area with their machetes. The rest of us joined them. Within minutes the hills resounded with the sounds of chopping wood and falling trees. As we began to work, an ominous rumble rolled through the darkening valley to the east, as if the mountain, suddenly aware of our presence, were rising to shake us from its side.

With the thunder came the first cold drops of a penetrating rain and a wave of frog sounds, high-pitched and strangely cheerful in the deepening twilight.

"Our brothers the frogs are laughing at our work," said someone in Shuar. It was Carlos, who, since the departure of Francisco and Calixto, had taken charge of the porter team. He was not often given to conversation, and I wondered if he meant something more by

88

the remark. If he too was losing patience with the light food and heavy loads, there would be even more trouble ahead.

Carlos made no further comment but began chopping at a large rotten stump near the center of the campsite. Suddenly he jumped back, staring at the ground in front of him. The leaves there were churning as if the rain had concentrated its force at a single point.

Teacup-size tarantulas were rushing from the base of the stump. They scurried under packs and between the stacks of cooking pots that stood at the edge of the newly made clearing. Carlos and several other Indians began slashing at the ground with their machetes as I dashed for my pack. I wanted to collect the spiders for the museum, but, by the time I could get a jar, most had disappeared.

"You're crazy," said Todd, when I crouched down and began sifting through the leaves and splintered wood with my hands. "Even if you don't get bitten, you're likely to get your fingers chopped off." Carlos and two of the other Indians were still savagely chopping wherever they saw hints of movement. I knew I would have to work quickly if I was to save anything. I pulled a small flashlight from my pocket and holding it in my teeth focused all my efforts at the base of the stump. The first spider I found was too large for the mouth of the jar. It crawled over my hands and between my feet. I had turned and was reaching for it a second time when Carlos's machete split it in half just inches from my fingers. The heavy steel blade sank deep into the sodden ground.

The tarantulas' graceful, fluid movements made the wild commotion they had caused seem strangely out of place. Before the fray was over, I had successfully eased two into separate collecting jars. The rest had escaped or been chopped to pieces in the growing darkness.

The rain had stopped by morning, and while Mark and Tom went out to look for new birds, Skip, Todd, and I strung nets on the ridges near camp. Two of the Indians were sent ahead to continue cutting a trail to the top of the mountain. The rest returned to Yapitya camp to retrieve the remaining equipment.

When they returned that evening, they reported the rivers swollen with the night's rain. The Rio Intsintsa, which the day before had been only waist deep, was now over the shoulders of the men. The clothing and equipment they carried would be wet for some time.

An Indian named Lucho, who had remained at Yapitya camp to guard our things, arrived with a special present. Tied into the tails of his sodden shirt were four squirming frogs he had caught at the river. One had a particularly beautiful leopard-spot pattern of brown and tan. It was, he assured me, especially good to eat. I thanked him for the thought, but explained that I would prefer to save it for the museum. He looked disappointed at the waste of such a delicacy.

In the interests of food rationing, we had been keeping a close watch on the passing days, but, as is often the case in the wild, we paid little attention to which day of the week was which and how it corresponded to the calendar holidays at home. It was, therefore, a delightful surprise when Skip announced that he had a treat in store for the evening. "Today is the Fourth of July," he announced, "and we're going to have some fireworks!"

Somehow, in all the trip preparations, Skip had thought to pack two boxes of sparklers for use on the expedition. That they had survived the rigors of the trail seemed hard to believe.

By nightfall, we had double reason to celebrate, for Mark had discovered an extremely rare bird with an intriguing name and an equally unusual story. The Masked Saltator he brought into camp just before dusk was only the second of its kind ever found in Ecuador.

"The first Masked Saltator any ornithologist ever saw was bought from a Shuar hunter near Macas more than forty years ago," explained Mark as he held out the small blue-gray bird for us to see. "That specimen was known to have come from the Cutucu, but until now, no one has dared enter these mountains to find it in its native haunts."

After all the difficulties we had had in getting here, Mark's saltator find was a welcome indication that "Tarantula camp" and the others still to come would be worth the struggle. "The higher we climb in the Cutucu, the more distinctive the habitat becomes," he observed. "This is where we are most likely to find the rarest birds." I knew the same was true of other animal groups, for we had already collected a number of insects, toads, and frogs seen nowhere else in our travels.

The nights were cooler here at 6,500 feet than earlier in the trip. A sweater felt good against the damp of the evening. A dinner of steaming rice and onion soup helped ease the exhaustion of the day.

"It's time for sparklers," announced Skip as we stacked the last of our metal soup bowls by the now-empty cooking pots.

"Let's do this carefully," warned Todd. "I don't think the Shuar have ever seen sparklers before. I'll try to explain what we're going to do."

Todd began by telling them a little about the United States, where it was and what it stood for. His words were carefully translated from Spanish to Shuar by the few men who could speak both languages. Finally he came to the subject of independence.

"We celebrate the day our country gained its independence from Great Britain," he explained. There was no reaction. "When does Ecuador celebrate its independence from Spain?" he asked, trying to involve them in his talk.

Este están bailondo con la musica de Tambor
Shuar

Japitia
Cutúcu

este es echo Dibujo por Pepe   Antum N

este   estan bailando con la   musica guitarre
Shuar

The woman pictured here presents her husband with a bowl of alcoholic drink made by chewing manioc root and spitting it into the bowl where it ferments for several days before it is consumed.

Drums, guitars, and shell-rattle belts provide the music for the ceremony in this Shuar drawing. Small crosses on their necks show that these Indians have had some contact with Christian missionaries.

An awkward silence followed. The Indians looked at each other in puzzlement. Then, suddenly, everyone was speaking at once. Some stated that the Shuar had always been independent. Others spoke of the tyranny of any government trying to impose its will on the people. Some, with a passing knowledge of Ecuador's history, suggested dates marking various battles or revolutions in the nation's past. Still others recounted bits of tribal history or family stories of freedom from famine or poor health. Most could not relate the concept of independence to a time or place. It was a sobering lesson, for us, on the way others view what we often take for granted.

"Let's forget the history and get on with the fun," interrupted Todd when the arguing got out of hand. With suitable ceremony, Skip handed one sparkler to each person. Together we tipped them toward the glowing embers of the fire.

As the damp sparklers sputtered to life, some of the Indians dropped them and ran from the fire with cries of fear. The rest, though frightened at first, quickly entered the spirit of the occasion. They laughed and cheered with us, swirling their flaming wands in circles through the darkness of the camp. I have celebrated independence in many ways, but no Fourth of July has ever been more memorable than the one spent in the Cutucu.

"If anyone's watching us tonight, they've certainly seen a show they won't soon forget," Todd said, laughing, as we readied for bed.

"Do you think we're being watched?" I asked, peering into the blackness.

"If we are," he answered, "tonight's fireworks may have done more to protect us than anything else we could have arranged."

Ambush

As our food supplies dwindled, all of us grew noticeably thinner and more tired. I tried to save my strength for the long trek out by resting each afternoon. Even that did little to counter the growing effects of malnutrition and fatigue brought on by our weeks in the jungle. Though we seldom discussed it, each of us wondered about the Shuar threat of violence and how it might affect the expedition's final days.

We knew that a similar group of American scientists had been attacked in an area near the Cutucu just a few years before. That expedition had not been as lucky as ours, for they had not learned of their danger until it was too late. Thoughts of their experience were never far from our minds.

As our expedition entered its final week, we found ourselves immersed in the complex logistics of feeding and housing our far-flung crew. Carlos and four of the Indian *macheteros*—machete men—were cutting new trails a full day's hike from our present camp. With their help we were still hoping for a final dash to the "top" of the Cutucu. If we made it, the trip would be more symbolic than practical. Our food supplies would not permit the extended camp and netting operations we had hoped for.

Todd had counted our provisions to the last cup of rice. It was clear from his calculations that if any of us were to make it to the top and still have food enough for the trek back to Logroño, some of us would have to leave before the last ascent. Such a divided exit would make each smaller group more vulnerable, but it might also permit a less conspicuous withdrawal and improve our chances of avoiding the Shuar.

There was only one trail as far as the Chiguaza River. It was the one we had cut oursleves. Carlos told us that from there we could find another way back to the swinging bridge that spanned the Upano River, separating Jívaro country from the settled lands beyond. He offered to lead us on a high hunting trail that would skirt the Shuar villages and keep us from the worst of the mud. The route would be longer and more difficult, but safer for us. We would not be expected on this trail, and if we traveled at night when Shuar warriors were most afraid of spirits, snakes, and jaguars, we might well reach the border undetected.

Todd and I agreed to forego the summit and take our chances with the Shuar. In the interests of the remaining group, we agreed to take no tents, hoping to do what sleeping we could under the shelter of abandoned Shuar lean-tos. We carried what was left of our clothes and enough food for two meals. Mark offered us shotguns, but we declined, convinced that, should we meet the Shuar, guns would only add to the tension. Carlos would have his own musket, but I would rather rely on Todd's language skills than arms to get us to Logroño.

Mark, Skip, and Tom were on hand to wish us well

as we began our long hike to the border. We had come to depend on each other during our weeks in the field. Now after two months we were splitting to go separate ways. Each wondered how the others would fare. It was a more difficult parting than I had expected. Then, with a round of handshakes and "good lucks" we were on our way.

Todd and I walked separately for a while, each lost in our own thoughts about ourselves, our homes, the expedition, and the difficult days ahead. Later we sought each other's company, talking of everything from birds to music, from good books to good food.

Late in the afternoon of our first day, Carlos, who generally kept well ahead of us, stopped at a river crossing to search the rocks for fish. I recognized the steep trail that led up the far bank, for we had passed this way before.

"If I stop now I'll never get to the top of the next hill," I explained to Todd, trudging through the waist-deep water. "I'll set my own pace and wait for you where the trail levels out."

The roar of the river faded behind me, and the afternoon moved quickly to dusk. Then a series of raspy buzzing cries filled the darkening forest. I moved silently closer, drawn by the mysterious sounds. Then, as suddenly as it had begun, the buzzing stopped. I stopped too and stood silent for a while, straining to see what had caused the noise. Then I edged on. When the sounds began again, I was just below their center. There in a tangle of tree limbs, not ten yards from where I stood, were eight brilliant orange birds vibrating their wings in unison. I had stumbled upon one of the rarest and most spectacular sights in the South American tropics, a Cock-of-the-Rock lek.

Before leaving the expedition, Frank Gill had told me about leks. "They are the secret meeting place of certain birds," he explained. "Here the male Cock-of-the-

The author jumps from rock to rock across a rain-swollen river. Some streams would rise by several feet after each rain.

Rocks gather to show off their plumage. The much drabber yellow-green females fly by and select their mates from the competing bachelors." So shy and rare are these birds that their leks are rarely seen. I felt like an invisible intruder.

The volume and pace of the buzzing grew with the arrival of several more birds, then rose to a frenzy with the approach of a curious hen. Each male bird was the size of a pigeon, but bright orange with black wings and tail and a large orange crest. The last rays of the setting sun lit their fiery plumage with spotlight intensity. Then, suddenly, they stopped their chorus and hurriedly dispersed. Todd and Carlos, following me up the trail, had disturbed the secret gathering. Only the croaking of frogs continued, filling the night with their eerie calls.

Most of the trip out was uneventful except for the occasional sightings of other unusual birds. The Shuar seemed not to have expected our coming. When we did meet them, it was they more than we who were taken by surprise.

In the afternoon of the final day, Carlos's high hunting trail joined a path more often traveled. It was the first of a series of confluences that would eventually lead to the Upano bridge. As usual, Carlos had rushed ahead and was nowhere to be seen. Todd and I, exhausted from four days of grueling travel, walked sluggishly along the winding, muddy path. Then, suddenly, turning a blind corner, we found ourselves facing three young Shuar warriors. Each carried a machete. As we tried to pass, they moved abreast of one another, blocking the way. Then began a lengthy

Many Cutucu trails become gooey trenches with mud as thick as peanut butter.

exchange. Though they addressed their questions and comments to me, it was Todd who did the talking, for I cannot speak Shuar.

Were we the gringos who were in the mountains looking for gold? they asked. "We have no gold," answered Todd. What were we doing in Shuar land? they wanted to know. Todd did his best to explain, but the answer failed to satisfy. More questions were asked and answers demanded. The tone of the three was increasingly hostile. It was clear from their staggering stance and raised voices that they had been drinking.

Finally the leader stepped forward, slapping my chest with the flat side of his machete. Why does this man not answer our questions? he demanded in words I could not understand. The situation was deteriorating badly. Their initial confusion had turned to cockiness and now bordered on violence.

"They are angry because they think you are snubbing them," explained Todd in a calm, low voice.

I needed no translation to know they were looking for a fight. "Tell them I am sick and trying to reach a doctor on the *colono* side of the border," I instructed, without taking my eyes from the central figure of the group.

Todd began.

"Tell them what I have is very contagious," I added. "We do not want to be responsible for spreading a deadly disease."

Todd's words had a powerful effect. As he spoke, the three men backed away as one, looking at me with widened eyes.

We stepped slowly past them and down the narrow trail.

"Don't look back," I advised as we walked on with measured pace. For a while I imagined pursuing footsteps, but it was only the pounding of my heart.

"We've got to make it to Logroño tonight," said Todd

during a break some hours later. "There is no safe place to camp here, and this trail will be crawling with Indians by morning."

I knew he was right. Fortunately the weather had broken in our favor. The sky was clear, and a nearly full moon now washed the trail with light. Since sundown we had been less worried about meeting more Indians than twisting our ankles on the uneven trail. Now at least we could tell where the weaving path led by the reflections from its watery surface.

I was beginning to wonder how much farther I could push myself, when at last the Upano River and its great swinging bridge came into view. We felt like cheering but were too tired to make a sound.

"I'm going to stop for another rest," I told Todd, removing my pack and slumping down on a rotting tree trunk. "You can go on ahead if you want, but wait for me on the other side of the river." The bridge was still a quarter of a mile ahead, but clearly visible above the Upano's surface. I knew that Logroño, the frontier town from which we had departed some six weeks before, was still several miles away. I would need all the strength I could muster to reach it.

Todd paused for a minute and looked back and forth between the sitting log and the bridge.

"I guess I'll keep going," he said at last, speaking more to himself than to me. His voice was barely audible above the river's steady roar.

I sat for a while in the semidarkness thinking of the highs and lows of this expedition that was now coming to an end. I thought too of the difficulties ahead. Though Logroño lay well within *colono* territory, I worried about the reception we might receive there. Would our disgruntled mule drivers be waiting to demand more pay for their work at the start of the expedition? Would Calixto and Francisco be there, eager to settle a score? Might there be Indians still hoping for a chance at the reward offered by Shuar leaders for attacking us? Where was Carlos now, and would he stay by us when the chips were down? Could we find food and lodging? If so, how soon could we eat and sleep? It was hunger that finally brought me to my feet again. For weeks I had dreamed of milk and crackers, chicken, eggs, fresh vegetables, ice cream and cake. Now such luxuries seemed almost within reach. I slung my camera bags and backpack over my shoulders and trudged slowly toward the bridge.

I had come to within ten feet of its rough wooden planks when a figure burst from the underbrush and faced me. A strongly built Shuar of nineteen or twenty, naked save for a pair of ragged shorts, stood in the path. He did not return my forced smile of greeting.

"*Buenas noches,*" I said, hoping that he might understand a Spanish geeting and forgive my trespass on Shuar lands. He replied in his own language with the same angry tones used by the three men we had encountered earlier in the day. Most of what he said was drowned by the roar of the river, but even if I had heard clearly, his words would have meant nothing to me.

I nodded and smiled and tried to pass, but he moved to block my way, raising his voice and repeating his unintelligible demands. We stood for an instant toe to toe. Then, as I tried to step around him, he grabbed the shoulder straps of my pack, pounding his fists into my chest, and knocking me backward with the force of the blow.

I glanced across the darkness of the bridge in hope that Todd or Carlos might come to my rescue. But I realized that the river's noise would cover even my loudest shout, and with the far bank more than a hundred yards away, they could not see us in the darkness.

The Indian was not carrying a machete, and if he had one hidden by the trail I did not want to give him a chance to reach it. Grabbing his wrists and setting one heel firmly in the mud, I spun suddenly to the left, swinging him with me, at the same time wrenching his hands from my pack. The action caught him off balance, and he staggered backward. As he struggled to regain his balance on the slippery rutted trail, I lunged forward, throwing the force of my weight and pack against his chest. It was enough to send him reeling backward toward the steep muddy bank of the river. His mouth was open and arms outstretched as he skidded over the edge, but I could not hear his cry. I had already turned and was running across the huge swaying bridge to safety.

The author, Mark Robbins, and Skip Glenn display the
expedition flag deep in the forbidden jungles of the Cutucu.

Afterword

For Todd and me the expedition that had started in La-
groño some six and a half weeks before would end
there within a few hours of the ambush at the Upano
bridge. Less than a week later Mark, Tom, Skip, and
the rest of the porter team made their own way to the
border. Well armed and traveling in force, with Carlos
again in the lead, they arrived in Logroño without in-
cident.

When we see each other now, we don't talk much
about the leaving—uneventful in their case, somewhat
less so in ours. What we do discuss are the extraordi-
nary things we saw together: vast tracts of wilderness
stretching beyond sight and past imagination, rain and
sun and rushing streams, tiny tree frogs, brilliant orchids, and tarantulas the size of teacups, land snails as
big as rats, muddy trails, elfin forests. And then there
were the birds. . . .

For Further Reading

Acosta-Solis et al. *Ecuador: In the Shadow of the Volcanoes.* Quito, Ecuador; Editiones Libri Mundi (World Wildlife Fund). 1982.

Blassingame, Wyatt. *The Incas and the Spanish Conquest.* New York; Julian Messner. 1980.

Carpenter, Allan. *Ecuador.* Chicago, Illinois; Children's Press. 1969.

Carter, William E. *South America;* revised edition. New York; Franklin Watts, Inc., 1983.

Harner, Michael J. *The Jivaro: People of the Sacred Waterfalls.* Published for the American Museum of Natural History; Garden City, New York; Doubleday/ Natural History Press, 1972.

Man, J. *Jungle Nomads of Ecuador: Waorami.* Peoples of the Wild Series. New York; Time-Life Books. Silver Burdett. 1982.

May, Charles. *Peru, Boliva, Ecuador; the Indian Andes.* Nashville, Tenn.; Thomas Nelson. 1969.

Sumwalt, Martha. *Ecuador in Pictures.* New York; Sterling Publishers. 1969.

Trupp, Fritz. *The Last Indians: South America's Cultural Heritages.* Perlinger. 1981.

About the Author

Naturalist, journalist, photographer, and historian, Robert McCracken Peck is a Fellow of The Academy of Natural Sciences of Philadelphia. He has participated in scientific expeditions to Asia, Africa, and South America and has traveled in such far places as Nepal, Kenya, Venezuela, Brazil, and the Galapagos Islands.

Peck was born and lives in Philadelphia. He has a B.A. in Art History and Archaeology from Princeton University and an M.A. in American Cultural History from the University of Delaware.

In his travels, Robert Peck has retraced the exploration routes of several early American naturalists. He has written about these trips and other research activities for such periodicals as *Audubon, National Wildlife, International Wildlife, The New York Times, The Philadelphia Inquirer, Omni, Image, American Art Review, Antiques, Arts,* and *FMR.*

The young naturalist's own color slides and black-and-white photographs chronicle his expeditions and illustrate his many professional lectures and school programs, as well as his books and articles.

Peck is the author of the highly acclaimed *A Celebration of Birds; The Life and Art of Louis Agassiz Fuertes,* published by Walker and Company in 1982.

Besides his own publications, Peck has written introductions for other natural history works and acted as a consultant to David Attenborough and the BBC.

Index

111

The Andes :
These Mountains are snow covered all year round although they are only a few degrees south of the Equator

Mt Sanga is an active volcano, 17,450 f

MACAS

Blowguns, usually 7 feet long, are used with poisoned darts to hunt for small game

SUCUA

Temporary C to store aband supplies

Mule drivers abandon us here

The Expedition starts here. Mules hired.

LOGRONO

Horse rolls downhill and is left for "El Tigre"

Jivaro village

Spider's Web of Slippery Trails

Scalp-lock Cabin

The Alternate Return Route

Campsite

The Bridge into the land of The Jivaro

River Upano

Cordillera de Condo 8000

EXPEDITION TO THE CORDILLERA DE CUTUCU ~ THE MOUNTAINS OF MOSS

Light easterly winds from the Amazon bring almost daily rain — up to 150 inches per year.

Summit Camp and Elfin Forest 8000 ft

Camp at 2225 M

The Cordillera de Cutucu is one of the few unexplored areas of the world. It is difficult to reach and equally difficult to leave.

Where we receive a death threat

Tarantula Camp

of Colono ers leave are

We eat the lips of rock-suckers

quasa Camp

Yapitya Camp

Yapitya Overlook the home of the secretive Highland Jivaron

The Author steps on the deadly bushmaster

In the heart of the Cordillera de Cutucu live the Jivaro Indians who revolted against the Spanish in 1599 and have since remained unconquered in their forest fastness

Small airfield for mission planes

YAUPI

ECUADOR
PERU

Disputed Border
Protocol of Rio de Janeiro, 1942 Declared null by Ecuador

: 1986 .

Santiago River to Marañon River

508.866
Pec

Peck, Robert
McCracken.

Headhunters and
hummingbirds : an
expedition into
Ecuador. $16.48

DATE DUE	BORROWER'S NAME	ROOM NO.
	L Cooley 10-21-88	
FE 20 '90	1 ay Rivard 1-30-90	
MAY 5 '93	Steve bermudez 7	